365

vie ways to be CONFIDENT

C000242171

Confidence comes from knowing yourself, improving your relationships with others and nourishing your mind, body and soul. Consider the bigger picture. Approach everything with an open mind and you will start to feel better about yourself as a whole, and as a result more at ease and confident.

**2**

Confidence isn't something you are born with; it's a state of mind that you can learn to acquire.

Whatever you want to achieve, get started now. Making the first step will give you the confidence you need to continue.

**4** Don't let the fear of failing stop you from ever getting started.

**5** Don't wait for everything to be perfect, because that day might never come.

**6** Start small. Your confidence will grow little by little.

**An idle mind has time to worry about all the things that could go wrong. Keep it busy and stay focussed.**

Just change one small thing for the better. It will trigger ripples that will impact other areas of your life.

**9**

Set yourself a small, achievable goal and go for it. The small wins will give you the confidence to tackle the bigger goals.

It's crazy how one thing can lead to another. Before you know it, you're achieving the impossible.

Write a list of things you feel confident about...

... compile a list of the areas of your life where
you most need to build confidence...

... make a note of goals you want to achieve.

Keep your three lists in mind as you work through the tips in this book. It will help you to stay focussed and serve as a reminder of the things you feel good about already. At regular intervals reassess your lists – tick off any goals you have achieved and add any new things that you feel confident about.

**15**

Feeling uncomfortable in a new situation is normal. It's a good thing, because it means you are giving yourself the chance to grow.

**16**

With uncertainty comes new experiences and new opportunities, and with new opportunities come new ways to build your confidence. A win–win situation.

**17**

Embrace the "un-comfort" zone.

**18**

Try something new every day.

**19**

Do something every day that scares you.

Build up your resilience by stepping outside of your comfort zone more frequently. Each time you do, you'll increase your tolerance for uncertainty. It may be hard at first, but the rewards in the end will be worth it. Start by trying new things – new foods, new routes to work, or push the boundaries with things that really challenge you.

# 21

Learn a new skill or take up a new activity.

# 22

It takes courage to be a beginner again, and research has shown that people who continue to learn throughout life are more optimistic and have a higher sense of self-worth.

Take a cooking class. The more you cook,
the better your food will taste.

**Learn a new language.**

Pick up an artistic hobby such as calligraphy,
life-drawing, or paper-craft.

Try a drama class. You will learn how to improvise and communicate clearly.

Learn to play a musical instrument. It's proven to raise your IQ!

Travel independently. You will learn to rely totally on yourself.

**29** Volunteer in your community. If you are helping out, people will see you in a positive light, which, in turn, will help you view yourself more positively.

**30** Join a choir. Hearing your own singing voice can be disconcerting, but when you do it as part of a group your confidence will grow.

**31**

Try your hand at crosswords or sudoku.
It will stimulate your mind, and you'll get a sense
of satisfaction every time you complete a puzzle.

**32**

Use online tutorials to complete a
DIY project – you'll get an enormous
kick out of completing the job.

Set yourself a weekly confidence challenge.
Pick one from the following pages or make up your own.
The sense of achievement you'll feel on completing
these challenges will bolster your confidence.

**34**

Go out for a meal alone.

 **35**

The next time you are in a meeting, ask a question.

 **36**

Memorize the route to a place you've never been
and walk there without consulting your map.

Go to the cinema or theatre alone.

**37**

**38**

Volunteer to give a presentation at work.

Ask someone out on a date. (It could be a "friend date" if you're in a relationship.)

**39**

**40** Introduce yourself to a stranger.
This could be at an event
or in an everyday situation,
like waiting at a bus stop.

Wear something that gets
you noticed – maybe a new
hat or a bright colour.

**42**

The next time there is a problem with your food
when eating out, make a polite complaint.

**43**

Travel somewhere you've never been
before by public transport.

**44**

Haggle for goods at a local market.

Be prepared. There are many situations in life where preparation can go a long way toward making you feel equal to the task at hand: whether that means preparing answers to questions for an interview or simply memorizing the route from the airport to your accommodation when you first arrive in a foreign country.

If you're feeling overwhelmed, take some of the pressure off by planning your day in advance.

Make your lunch the night before.

Write a to-do list of tasks to complete during the day.

**49**

Empower yourself with knowledge. Read a book on a subject that you know nothing about

 **50**

Study the greats in your chosen subject area.

 **51**

Aim high. You might just get there.

**52** Jump in and give it a try. People learn best by doing.

**53** Practise. It is only by repetition that your competence – and confidence – will increase over time.

**54** Celebrate every win.

**55**

Take frequent breaks to allow your brain to recharge. Try using the Pomodoro technique: work for 25 minutes, rest for 5 minutes.

**56**

Test yourself. Recapping reinforces knowledge, and you'll get the confidence boost of seeing how much you've already learned.

**57**

Talk to others who are going through the same thing. You will gain solidarity and new insights, too.

**58**

Reinforce your knowledge by teaching others.

**59**

Practise what you're bad at. By practising what you're good at, you stay in your comfort zone.

Be mindful when you practise. If you don't concentrate, your session will be less useful.

**61** Remember that improvement takes time.

Write a "Did-it" list. Seeing a list of your achievements will boost your confidence.

Immediately prior to undertaking something that you've been preparing for, such as a driving test or presentation, it's perfectly natural for the nerves to kick in and to panic that you haven't done enough preparation. In this moment, try to focus on all the work you have done to prepare for the event, instead of what you haven't done.

# 64

Write down good things about your
life on "positive sticky notes" and
stick them up around your home...

... and when you're having a bad day,
look at the sticky notes for a reminder
of everything that's good in your life.

What we think, we become. Negative thoughts
lead to a negative mind; positive to a positive.

**The first step toward getting what you
want is to start believing you can have it.**

Pay less attention to what other people think
and whether things will go well or not.

Don't take yourself too seriously.
Admit your mistakes and laugh at yourself.

Make a playlist full of power
songs that make you feel good.

Face your fears. Feel fear,
but don't let it get in the way.

# 72

Believe that you can do it. If you approach a task believing that you will fail, you are likely to tackle it half-heartedly.

# 73

Embrace your child self. When we're young, we think we can conquer the world; it is only as we get older that we accumulate self-limiting beliefs.

**74**

Think of an "impossible" goal and start to plan how to achieve it.

**75**

Clear your mind of "can't" and the fears that hold you back and simply be in the present.

**76**

Trust yourself and move forward.

Humans are hardwired to see anything new or different as a threat to their survival; a useful instinct back in the caveman days, when it was often a case of get lunch or be lunch. But in our modern world, not every new experience is to be feared. To gain confidence we must overcome this inbuilt "negativity bias". To do this, follow the process on the following pages.

For every negative thought, think
of five positive ones to counter it...

... Consider each of these positive thoughts for
20 seconds before moving on to the next one...

... Acknowledge any emotions that arise,
whether good or bad...

... Do not try to suppress the negative emotions...

... Once you have labelled these emotions for what they are, move on...

... Repeat this process every time you encounter a new experience to defeat the negativity bias.

**84**

Keep a confidence diary – write down the
highs and the lows. When you're having a low,
you can look back at some of the highs.

**85**

Did you know that the human brain and body
are unable to distinguish between something real and
imagined? Imagine yourself succeeding, and you will.

If you want something, ask for it with
the confidence that you deserve it.

**Remember that worrying serves no purpose.**

Courage isn't about not feeling afraid;
it's about feeling the fear and going for it anyway.

**89**

Think about one of your heroes.
You probably see them as eternally
brave, but even they experience
moments of fear and doubt.

When you are confident, you will be calm;
when you lack confidence, you are likely
to become nervous. Try to stay calm; it will
tend to help you feel more confident.

Turn "I can't" into "I can".

Carry a lucky charm. Indulging your superstition
could give you the confidence to perform well.

Instead of focussing on skills you don't have,
focus on skills you are acquiring.

Do the impossible. It doesn't have to be dangerous or something insanely physically challenging – just something you secretly always wished you could do but told yourself you couldn't. By completing the challenge you will have to admit that you were wrong about it being impossible and maybe you'll start to view other "impossible" goals as within your reach.

Play. There is no right or wrong way.
Embrace this creative freedom.

There's no such thing as a bad
idea. Every creative project
has to start somewhere.

Don't wait for inspiration to strike.
Just try something. Anything.

You don't have to please everyone. Create because you enjoy creating, and know that there will be those who get it and those who don't.

Practise your art. The more often you use your creativity, the faster your creative confidence will grow.

Take some time out to
get to know yourself.

Accept yourself for who you are,
and the world will accept you.

There is no one who can tell you
who to be except yourself.

**103**

If you are self-aware, it is easier for you to
understand other people and how they perceive
you. It also creates the possibility for change.

**104**

**Think about the principles you want to live
by and never hesitate to follow them through.**

**105**
Trust yourself and the decisions you make.

**106**
Know that if things go wrong, you will know what to do to handle the situation.

**107**
Consider your unique gifts and what you can offer to the world.

Make your goals about you. Society has a way of making us feel that there are certain things we should aspire to have and do. But you will never find the motivation to complete a task if your heart's not in it. Think about what you really want in life and go for it!

Write down a list of your strengths.

Identify your weaknesses and keep them clearly in mind.

Don't be tempted to avoid your weak areas. You will never get any better until you try.

# T12

Ask the people you most trust to compile a list of your strengths and weaknesses. You might be pleasantly surprised and gain some insight.

# 113

Ask for some formal feedback at work. Once the process is finished, reflect on it by writing down your main takeaways.

Keep a mood diary to record times
when your confidence takes a dive.

Make an action plan to avoid these triggers.

If a certain person always makes negative comments
about you, limit your contact with them.

Make self-care a part of your weekly routine,
even when you're super busy.

Be patient, loving and gentle with yourself.

Be your own best friend.
Treat yourself fairly and with integrity.

## 120

Travelling alone is a great way to get to know your needs and motivations.

## 121

Take a personality assessment, such as the Myers–Briggs or DISC personality profile. The results can provide a useful structure for understanding your behaviour and working style.

**122**

Journaling can help you to get to know yourself better.
Find some quiet time each day to write down your thoughts,
whatever they may be – they don't necessarily need to be
related to your goals. Nobody ever has to read what you write,
so write honestly and freely. Putting thoughts into words
forces them to crystallize and will bring you better clarity.

## 123

Write down everything you want to create and have in your life. Seeing your goals written down on paper will help to make them feel more real.

## 124

When journaling, you could try thinking about some of the prompts on the following page.

What is important to me right now?

125

126

What are my values?

127

What things make me feel truly happy?

**128**

Notice your inner critic: the voice in your head that says negative things.

**129**

Keep an inner critic log. Note the times and situations when it pipes up.

**130**

Once you are aware of how your inner critic operates, you can stand up to it.

You weren't born with an inner critic.
It is a voice that came from outside.

**See yourself as distinct from your inner critic.**

Give your inner critic a silly name to reduce its potency.

**134**

Narrate your inner rants as though they were fairy tales. It will help you to see them for what they are: stories you tell yourself.

When you catch yourself thinking a negative thought, say "Abort thought!" and think about something else.

**135**

**136** Answer back. Tell your inner critic you don't want to hear what it has to say.

**137** Replace your inner critic with an inner cheerleader.

**138** Ask yourself what your best friend would say to you.

**139**

Learn to self-edit. Words are powerful,
and a small tweak can change everything.

**140**

Reach for the facts in any situation. Instead of
thinking "I'm useless at running", think "I want to
run a 5K. I know of a training app I can try".

**141**

The next time something goes wrong, replay the scenario. You will see more clearly all the contributing factors and realize not all of them were down to you.

**142**

Write down three of your frequently occurring negative thoughts. Next to each one, write down the positive opposite.

Start to question your beliefs about yourself. If you often find yourself saying "I will never be able to do X", ask yourself "Why will I never be able to do X?" Try to come up with five answers to that question. If the only response you can make is "Because I'm not good enough", then you have to admit that your logic is faulty.

# 144

Write affirmations down on sticky notes and display them around your home, where you will be reminded of them every day.

145

Phrase your affirmations in the present tense, as if you are already grateful for having what you describe.

Repeat positive affirmations
to yourself on a daily basis.

Keep your affirmations short
and easy to remember.

On the following pages are some ideas
for affirmations to get you started.

**149**

"I am competent and capable."

 **150**

"I am flexible and open to new experiences."

 **151**

"I am loved and respected wherever I go."

**152**

"I am free to choose to live as I wish."

**153**

"I know who I am."

"I am enough."

**154**

**155**

"I choose to be present in all that I do."

**156**

"I choose to think thoughts that serve me well."

**157**

"I share my happiness with those around me."

"I feel energetic and alive."

"I know with time and effort
I can achieve anything."

"I love challenges and what
I learn from overcoming them."

Give yourself a pep talk. In their training,
US Navy SEALS are taught to speak positively
to themselves. This helps them to override fears
resulting from the limbic brain system, a primal part
of the brain that helps us to deal with anxiety.

**162**

Praise yourself whenever you complete a task.

**163**

Make a list of ten things you like about yourself.

**164**

Use positive words about others. If you are negative about others you are more likely to be negative about yourself.

**165**

Stop predicting catastrophes, the "what ifs" and "maybes", and focus on the task in hand.

**166**

Let go of regrets. We've all done things we're not proud of.

**167**

Recognize that, despite what you might think, not everyone is thinking bad thoughts about you.

**168**

The human brain is wired to seek answers to
questions. Turn your affirmations into questions
and your brain will accept them more readily.

**169**

If something embarrassing happens, tell someone.
In the retelling you'll soon see the funny side,
and it will no longer seem like a big deal.

**Avoid thinking in absolutes such as "always" and "never". Try to see the bigger picture.**

Often our worries are abstract; when we really think about it, we realize we have the tools we need to deal with anything.

Don't compare your body to others'.

**72**

**73**

See yourself as equal to and
as deserving as others.

Take a break from social media, or at
least remember that it isn't reality.

**74**

Treasure compliments. Thank the person, write the compliment down and save it for a low point.

Celebrate what your body can do.

Be grateful to your body for the tough times it has got you through.

**178**

Always look your best.
*Your* best is good enough.

**179**

If you wouldn't say it to a friend,
don't say it to yourself either.

**180**

Know that other people are more likely to be worrying
about how they look than judging you.

Judging others leads to judging yourself. If you catch yourself thinking unkind thoughts about another person's appearance, stop and instead focus on something positive about them. By practising this in your thoughts about others, it will become easier to do it about yourself.

**182**

Declutter your wardrobe. Only keep clothes that fit and you feel good in.

**183**

Treat yourself to some new clothes. Choose colours that you love and that suit your skin tone.

**184**

Think about what the confident version of you would wear. Now wear that.

# 185

If your hair looks good, you look good. Revel in the confidence-boosting powers of a visit to the salon!

# 186

Take a break from the television. TV shows are filled with perfect-looking people, filling our heads with unrealistic expectations about appearances. Refocus on what is real.

Try to look like the winner you are destined to be.

**Never underestimate the power of positive body language!**

Learn the body signals that will make you appear more confident to others.

Make eye contact. It's a sign of trustworthiness
and will make you seem self-assured.

If you find making eye contact awkward, stare at the
spot between the other speaker's eyes – to them it will
still look as if you are maintaining direct eye contact.

**192**

Stand up straight and you'll feel ready to take on the world.

**193**

Keep your head held level to appear more poised and self-assured.

Celebrate successes with an exuberant air punch for a fix of happy vibes.

**194**

# 195

Nod your head. It's a form of affirmation in conversation, and a sort of self-validation — so use the gesture to affirm positive thoughts.

Uncross your arms and legs. It will make you appear more open and your body will take up more space, a known indicator of confidence.

Don't fiddle with your clothes and
hair or touch your face.

**Practise your handshake to get it right
– firm, but not too aggressive.**

Sit up straight.

**200**

Smile. A smile instantly makes you more attractive, likeable and approachable to others. When others see you in this way, it helps you to believe in yourself. Did you know that the physical action of smiling actually releases endorphins? Your mood will soon start to reflect the emotion that your facial expression is conveying, and a happier you is a more confident you.

**201**

Adopt a "power pose": shoulders squared, arms by the sides, feet hip-width apart.

**202**

Keep in touch with people. Small gestures of contact help to create a human bond.

**203**

Smile when you speak. It makes your voice more pleasant to listen to.

**204**

Take a step back. Research has shown that in a difficult situation, taking a step back can increase your ability to cope.

Use your hands to reinforce what you're saying. Speakers who use a variety of gestures are perceived to have warmth and energy.

**205**

**206**

Stop saying sorry. Only apologize when
it's actually really necessary.

**207**

Speak slowly and clearly...

**208**

... but not too slowly, or you risk
sending the listener to sleep!

**209**

When speaking in public, breathe in deeply
and breathe out from your stomach. Your voice will
resonate, giving you a deeper, calmer speaking voice.

**210**

Make statements, rather than asking questions.
A question can imply you are missing information
or want approval for an idea or decision.

## 211

Don't let your voice creep upward at the end of a sentence.

## 212

Know what you are going to say and why you want to say it.

## 213

Ditch redundant phrases. Say what you mean and nothing else.

# 214

Remember that what you have to
say is worth saying – and it's worth
other people's time to listen.

# 215

Before you speak in public, take a moment to
sit quietly, close your eyes and imagine yourself
giving your speech with resounding success.

Stay hydrated. It keeps your vocal cords moisturized
and enhances the sound of your voice.

**Practise speaking to a small supportive audience
where less is at stake, or in front of a mirror.**

Stand up and walk around as you practise out loud.

If you pitch the speed at which you speak right, your audience will feel less like you're talking at them and more like you're having a chat over lunch. Carmine Gallo, author of *Talk Like TED*, claims 190 words per minute is the ideal rate of speech for public speaking.

**220**

Imagine you're explaining your ideas to a friend.

**221**

Rather than focussing on yourself, focus on your audience.

**222**

Connect with your audience. Look them in the eye as you speak to them, one person at a time.

**223**

Don't memorize your speech word for word. Make an easy-to-remember list of things you will cover. Talk it through, point by point.

Remember to thank others for their contribution. Displaying gratitude shows that all is going well and inspires confidence in others.

**224**

Remember that even experienced
speakers get nervous.

Turn your jitters into energy
to enhance your delivery.

Keep it short and simple.
The golden rule is three key ideas.

**228**

Watch TED talks to observe how
confident speakers operate.

**229**

Insert strategic pauses into your speech
to allow your audience to digest key points.

**230**

The ability to be comfortable with silence
shows that you are confident and at ease.

## 231

Compliment a stranger without expecting
one in return, just so you can practise
approaching people you don't know.

## 232

Try putting your phone down once in a while.
Smartphones are marvellous inventions, but they can
also be a crutch and a hindrance to real-life interaction.

Next time you're in a shop or cafe, try being friendly and talkative with the person serving you. It's their job to talk to you, so that takes a little bit of the fear out of starting up a conversation. And you might just bring some joy to what might otherwise have been a boring day at work for them.

**234**

You can't be good at everything. Find others who are strong where you are weak and ask for their support.

**235**

Surround yourself with people who know how great you are.

**236**

If there are people in your life who don't buoy you up, it's OK to let them go.

Live by your word. Having a set of values, and sticking to them, will reaffirm your character.

**237**

**238**

Think in the long term. Address your problem fully and don't opt for a quick fix.

Look the part.

**239**

**240**

Be a good listener. It will help the other person
to feel valued and at ease, and the conversation
will flow more naturally as a result.

**241**

Be kind and generous to others. Knowing that
you bring something positive to the world can
increase your sense of self-worth.

**242**

If you disagree with something, speak up.
Calmly and kindly explain your opinion.

**243**

Be authentic. Don't make up stories or
try to act a certain way to impress.

**244**

Always be honest about how you feel.

**245**

Learn to say no. When you're lacking in confidence,
it's easy to fall into the trap of people-pleasing by saying yes
to everything. But this will actually reduce your confidence,
reinforcing the idea that the wishes of others are more
important than your own. Setting some personal boundaries
and being more assertive will help you to gain more control.

**246**

Evaluate your role in a relationship.
You will realize that your relationship is
solid and can withstand your saying no.

**247**

When you say no, the other person might
not accept it. Stand firm. Don't feel you have to
give in to prevent them feeling uncomfortable.

**248**

Simply say no. Don't beat around the bush or offer excuses.

**249**

When saying no, be assertive but courteous.

**250**

If someone is asking the impossible, don't be afraid to suggest a compromise.

Practise saying no in the following scenarios:

You're invited on a night out but you can't afford to go.

You're on a diet. Someone tries to pressure you to have dessert.

Someone asks you to house-sit for the weekend.

An old acquaintance you are not particularly
fond of invites themselves to stay.

It really is OK to be selfish sometimes. Practise putting
your needs first. It will get easier each time.

**257**

Make the most of your support network. Share your hopes and aspirations and you'll find your own personal band of cheerleaders waving you on.

If forced to spend time around someone who is stressed, don't absorb their mood. Counteract their negativity with positive statements.

**258**

**259**

Find a confidence role model. Spend time in
their company, observing how they behave.

**260**

Maintain your individuality, and some
independence, within a romantic relationship.

**261**

Do not accept unjustified criticism and negative behaviours.

**262**

Remember that the way someone treats you says
more about them than it does about you.

**263**

Don't overanalyze another person's actions.
Believe that you are worthy of being liked.

**264**

If a relationship ends, it's because it wasn't right,
not because there is something wrong with you.

## 265

Focus on the positive. Offer your partner compliments and reassurance and you will likely receive the same in return.

Share an embarrassing secret or story with your partner. Being vulnerable and open builds trust and confidence within your relationship.

## 266

Develop and treasure friendships
that you know you can rely on.

**267**

**268**

Don't be a show-off. You don't
need to sell yourself to anyone.

Accept responsibility for your actions
and emotions; do not blame others.

**269**

Everyone makes mistakes. If you feel insecure, it's easy to fall into the trap of walking on eggshells, worrying that you might do something to upset the other person. But if someone truly values you, they're not going to reject you just because you say or do one thing wrong. If they do, they're not worth having in your life anyway.

Know what you will and will not accept from others.

Never stay in a relationship that doesn't feel right.

Take some time to note down the things you
bring to the relationships in your life.

# 274

If you're on a date and feel nervous,
remember that the other person
is probably just as nervous, too.
Try to put them at ease.

# 275

Don't overthink a first date. Simply be open to the
experience and what it may (or may not) bring.

**276**

Find a quiet place of confidence through meditation.

**277**

Create a dedicated meditation space, somewhere calm and uncluttered in your home.

**278**

Try starting your day with a simple mindfulness meditation.

Find calm. Sit comfortably. Set a five-minute
timer on your phone. Close your eyes and focus
on the breath, breathing in through the nose,
out through the mouth. Notice how the chest
rises and falls with the breath. If your mind
wanders, gently bring it back to your breath...

**280**

... Use this technique to disassociate from any negative thoughts churning and to let go of obsessive thoughts about the past or the future...

**281**

As you go about your day, if you notice your mind slipping into a spiral of negative self-talk, take a minute to focus on the breath.

**282**

Make meditation a part of your daily routine.

**283**

Build your meditation practice; increase the duration and frequency over time.

**284**

Visualize a detailed image of a more confident you.

**285**

Incorporate exercise into your weekly routine.

**286**

Exercise releases endorphins: the happy hormones!

**287**

Find a way to exercise that you enjoy; picking an activity you enjoy will help keep you motivated.

**288**

Set yourself exercise goals. As you achieve each increasingly demanding physical task, your self-confidence will rise.

Some days you might not have the energy for a challenging workout. That's OK, just do what you can. Even five minutes is better than nothing.

**289**

**290**

The more you exercise,
the more energy you will have.

**291**

The more energy you have,
the stronger you will feel.

**292**

As a result of exercising, you'll start to have
a more positive relationship with your body.

Take lessons in a martial art. You'll get fit and feel more confident in yourself.

**293**

**294**

Try swimming: both a form of exercise and a way to unwind.

Give gardening a go. The fresh air will do wonders and you can feel proud of your garden!

**295**

## 296

Instead of feeling embarrassed when exercise makes you red-faced and sweaty, look at it as an encouraging sign that you're doing something right.

## 297

Consider joining a fitness club or taking up a team sport. You'll be motivated to exercise and may even make some new friends along the way.

Stay off the sad step. Focussing on weight as a means to measuring improvement in fitness can be misleading, as we can actually gain weight as we build muscle. If we don't achieve our "ideal weight" our confidence can take a hit. Instead, measure your success in terms of achieving goals, such as progressing to lift a heavier weight or completing a 5K run.

**299**

Remember that everyone
who exercises was once a beginner.

**300**

Focus on your own fitness journey;
don't compare yourself to others.

**301**

Every day is an opportunity to get fitter,
stronger and more confident.

**302**

Write "I'm working toward the confident new me!" on a piece of paper and stick it somewhere you will see it as you work out.

Make yourself accountable by keeping a fitness journal. Plan your sessions and tick off each one as you complete it.

**303**

Remember: to increase your fitness you have to push yourself beyond your comfort zone.

# 304

# 305

Set realistic targets. Start out small and work your way up.

Whenever you achieve a fitness target, congratulate your body!

# 306

**307**

Practise yoga to align your body and mind
and achieve a sense of calm well-being.

**308**

Eat a healthy, balanced diet full of nutrient-rich
foods. You will feel healthier overall and have the
energy you need to chase your dreams.

**309**

Include lots of mood-balancing and
mood-boosting B-vitamins in your diet.

**310**

Cut down on caffeine. It raises stress
levels and can lead to anxiety.

**311**

Try mood-boosting herbal drinks such
as ginseng, ginger and lemon teas.

# 312

Fat is not the enemy! Eating the right amount of healthy fats such as those found in avocados, olive oil, nuts and seeds helps toward having healthy skin.

## 313

It's been scientifically proven that dark chocolate can lift your mood, so treat yourself to some now and again – just don't go too crazy.

**314**

Eat fish. It's full of omega-3 fatty acids that help power your brain.

**315**

For healthy skin that glows, eat more antioxidant cucumber.

**316**

Drink plenty of water. Staying hydrated is essential for maintaining optimum energy!

Incorporate more lean proteins such as chicken, fish and tofu into your diet. They keep you feeling full for longer and contain amino acids, which help your body to produce serotonin, dopamine and noradrenaline which in turn balance your mood and make you feel more positive.

**318**

Enjoy the calming and soothing effects
of calcium, combined with vitamin D for mood
enhancement. Good sources of calcium are dairy foods,
leafy green vegetables, lentils, beans and Brazil nuts.

**319**

Like mother always said: eat your greens.
They're full of fibre for good digestion, rich
in iron, improving blood flow and circulation,
and a good source of serotonin.

**320**

Eat a banana for an instant hit of magnesium and phosphorus, which aid in the production of happy hormones.

**321**

Be consistent with nutrition and you will see results over time.

**322**

Dance – it can fill you with feel-good vibes.

**323**

Don't comfort eat. Sugary snacks give you a boost initially, but you'll feel worse when it wears off.

**324**

Eat slow-energy-release foods to give you the power to fight on.

**325**

Replace sugary snacks such as chocolate bars with naturally sweet foods.

**326**

Cut back on the booze. Thanks to alcohol's inhibition-repressing qualities, having a few drinks can make you feel more confident at first – but know that the effects will be short-lived. Common after-effects include anxiety and depression, which will lower your self-confidence even further. Worse, you can become reliant on this quick fix to feel comfortable in social situations. Aside from the bad effects alcohol can have on your health, it also means that you're avoiding the problem, rather than fixing it.

**327**

Take some time out to enjoy the great outdoors. Reconnecting with nature can bring a real sense of peace and tranquillity, giving you renewed energy.

Get a good night's rest. A rested mind is a healthy mind, better able to face the challenges of the day.

**328**

**329**

Try progressive relaxation to help you fall asleep. Start at your toes and work your way all the way up to the top of your head, clenching each body part in turn tightly, then release. Feel the tension melt away.

Make your bedroom a
sleep sanctuary, reserved
only for catching Zs.

**330**

**331**

Keep televisions, computers,
phones and other devices
out of the bedroom.

Burn lavender essential oil
to help you fall asleep.

**332**

**333**

Start your day right with a morning routine.
Make your first action a short mindfulness meditation.
Follow this up by setting your intentions for the day ahead.

**334**

You may not be able to control everything that
happens to you, but you can choose how you react.

**335**

When faced with an uphill struggle,
think of the view from the top.

**336**

Practise floating on your back in a swimming pool. To do this you must completely relax and let go, and have faith that the water will hold you up.

**337**

Take a long, hot soak in the bath. The warm water and scents of your favourite essential oils will help to ease away tension and restore calm.

**338**

Devote a day or evening to yourself and totally switch off from the world.

**339**

Write your worries down on a piece of paper, then throw it – and your worries – away.

**340**

Declutter to restore a sense of orderly calm and purpose to your home.

## 341

Take control of your finances. Cancel unnecessary services and cards, consolidate your debts and work out a monthly repayment plan and a monthly budget and stick to it.

## 342

Put money aside for doing things that make you happy, whether it's your favourite activity or spending time with friends.

**343**

Book an acupressure session to allow
your body's energy to flow freely.

**344**

Try reflexology to release blockages
and feel relaxed and balanced.

**345**

If your confidence issues are impacting
on your daily life, see a doctor.

**346**

When you're stuck in a rut, tackle a job that you've been avoiding for a long time – just by making a start you will get a quick boost and feel more inclined to complete it.

**347**

Focus on solutions rather than problems. Think about the skills you have that you can use to get the result you want.

**348**

Don't dwell on the past. If something went wrong, learn from it and move on.

**349**

Confidence is knowing what to do if mistakes happen.

**350**

Always have a backup plan.

**35**

Whenever something doesn't turn out as you hoped, write down the things you did right in the situation. Alongside the first, write a second list of things that could be done better the next time. Whenever something *does* turn out as you hoped, complete the same exercise. Keep these lists as a reminder that there is no such thing as failure or success; only an ongoing process of learning and improving.

# 352

Failure is a good thing.
Because it means you tried.

## 353

Take a moment and a few breaths and
remind yourself that you are capable.

## 354

Embrace criticism as an opportunity to grow and learn something new.

If things don't go according to plan, treat it as an opportunity to learn what you can do better next time.

## 355

**356**

When you hit a setback, ask yourself: will this still bother me in a week, month or year from now? Probably not. So don't take it to heart.

**357**

Listen carefully to any criticism and use it to your advantage.

**358**

Don't define yourself by other people's opinions of you.

**359**

Face your fear of criticism by exposing
yourself to situations where you may encounter it.

**360**

Never be afraid to ask for help if you are
feeling overwhelmed. Rather than being a sign
of weakness, it actually takes great courage
and strength to admit you need help.

# 361

The road to gaining confidence is a journey.
There will be twists and turns along the way,
but you will get there. Just keep on going.

# 362

As long as you keep trying, you will never fail.

# 363

The only way you can
fail is if you give up.

Go for it:
you've got this.

# 364

If you're interested in finding out more about our books, find us on Facebook at **Summersdale Publishers** and follow us on Twitter at **@Summersdale**.

**www.summersdale.com**

Nobody is perfect. Even as your confidence grows and you find success, remember that there is always more that you can learn. Be humble as you continue on your lifelong journey of self-growth.